Mr Top
Goes to the ZOO

GW01418934

written by Jay Dale

illustrated by Amanda Gulliver

"It's my birthday," said Mr Top.
"I want to go to the zoo."

"No!" said Mrs Top.
"I don't want to go to the zoo.
We HAVE to stay at home."

"Come on," said Mr Top.

"The sun is out and the sky is blue.

It's a good day to go to the zoo."

So Mr Top and Mrs Top
went to the zoo in their little car.
Brrmmmm! Brrmmmm!

There were lots of people at the zoo.

"Look at all the people,"
smiled Mr Top.
"They have come to the zoo, too.
It's a good day to go to the zoo."

Mrs Top could see lots of people out and about.

Everyone was having fun.

But Mrs Top was NOT having fun.

"Come on," said Mr Top.
"Let's go and see the monkeys.
I like the monkeys very much."

Mrs Top was just about to go
with Mr Top, when she stopped.
"No!" she said.
"I don't want to see the monkeys.
We HAVE to go home!"

"Come on," said Mr Top.
"Let's go and see the lions.
I like the lions very much."

Mrs Top was just about to go
with Mr Top, when she stopped.
"No!" she said.
"I don't want to see the lions.
We HAVE to go home!"

"Well," said Mr Top.

"I don't want to go home.

It's my birthday.

I want to stay at the zoo.

It's a good day to go to the zoo."

"No!" said Mrs Top.

"We have to go home.

We HAVE to go home right now!"

So Mrs Top and Mr Top
went home in their little car.
Brrmmmm! Brrmmmm!

Mr Top was not happy.

He was very cross.

"I don't want to go home," he said,

as he opened the door.

"Happy birthday!" shouted Mr Top's friends.